COOKING CHEMISTRY
HOW DOES BREAD RISE?

by Tracy Vonder Brink

pogo

Ideas for Parents and Teachers

Pogo Books let children practice reading informational text while introducing them to nonfiction features such as headings, labels, sidebars, maps, and diagrams, as well as a table of contents, glossary, and index.

Carefully leveled text with a strong photo match offers early fluent readers the support they need to succeed.

Before Reading

- "Walk" through the book and point out the various nonfiction features. Ask the student what purpose each feature serves.
- Look at the glossary together. Read and discuss the words.

During Reading

- Have the child read the book independently.
- Invite them to list questions that arise from reading.

After Reading

- Discuss the child's questions. Talk about how they might find answers to those questions.
- Prompt the child to think more. Ask: Have you ever thought about why bread dough rises? What other baking questions do you have?

Pogo Books are published by Jump!
3500 American Blvd W, Suite 150
Bloomington, MN 55431
www.jumplibrary.com

Copyright © 2026 Jump!
International copyright reserved in all countries. No part of this book may be reproduced in any form without written permission from the publisher.

Jump! is a division of FlutterBee Education Group.

Library of Congress Cataloging-in-Publication Data

Names: Vonder Brink, Tracy, author.
Title: How does bread rise? / by Tracy Vonder Brink.
Description: Minneapolis, MN: Jump!, Inc., [2026]
Series: Cooking chemistry | Includes index.
Audience: Ages 7-10
Identifiers: LCCN 2024060447 (print)
LCCN 2024060448 (ebook)
ISBN 9798892138314 (hardcover)
ISBN 9798892138321 (paperback)
ISBN 9798892138338 (ebook)
Subjects: LCSH: Bread—Analysis—Juvenile literature.
Classification: LCC TX769 .V65 2026 (print)
LCC TX769 (ebook)
DDC 664.7523—dc23/eng/20250131
LC record available at https://lccn.loc.gov/2024060447
LC ebook record available at https://lccn.loc.gov/2024060448

Editor: Katie Chanez
Designer: Anna Peterson

Photo Credits: Scrudje/Shutterstock, cover (top); wophovid/Shutterstock, cover (bottom); Jiri Hera/Shutterstock, 1; kungfu01/Shutterstock, 3; Imageman/Shutterstock, 4; Candice Bell/Shutterstock, 5; YuanruLi/iStock, 6; Pinkybird/iStock, 7; Pawel Michalowski/Shutterstock, 8-9; TAMER YILMAZ/iStock, 10-11; Mike Neale/Dreamstime, 12-13; blakisu/iStock, 14-15 (bread); Ground Picture/Shutterstock, 14-15 (kitchen); Antonova Ganna/Shutterstock, 16-17; Diane Labombarbe/iStock, 18 (recipe card); New Africa/Shutterstock, 18 (flour); Katie Chanez, 19-21; Africa Studio/Shutterstock, 21 (oven); Anna Chelnokova/Shutterstock, 23.

Printed in the United States of America at Corporate Graphics in North Mankato, Minnesota.

TABLE OF CONTENTS

CHAPTER 1
Bread Basics 4

CHAPTER 2
Bread Science 6

CHAPTER 3
Let's Bake! 18

ACTIVITIES & TOOLS
Try This! 22
Glossary 23
Index 24
To Learn More 24

CHAPTER 1
BREAD BASICS

Bread dough rises in a bowl. It puffs up. Soon it will be ready to bake!

dough

Bread is made by mixing and baking water and **grains**, such as wheat flour. The basic bread **ingredients** are flour, water, and salt. Many breads also have a **rising agent**, such as yeast.

salt

water

flour

yeast

CHAPTER 1

CHAPTER 2
BREAD SCIENCE

Flour is ground up grains or seeds. Wheat flour is often used to make bread. It has **proteins** and **starch**.

wheat

kneading

Flour changes when water is added to it. How? Water breaks down the flour's starch. It changes it to sugars. At the same time, the water and flour proteins form **gluten**. We **knead** dough. Why? This connects gluten **molecules**. They form a stretchy net. It gives bread its shape.

CHAPTER 2

Yeasts are simple living things. The kind used to make bread is often dried. When water is added, yeast eats the sugars. Then the yeast lets out **carbon dioxide**. This makes bubbles in the dough.

DID YOU KNOW?

Yeast helps dough rise. Baking soda and baking powder do, too. But they are not alive like yeast.

The bubbles push against the dough. Gluten traps them inside. This makes the dough rise.

TAKE A LOOK!

How does bread dough rise? Take a look!

1 Two flour proteins and water mix. They form gluten.

PROTEIN + PROTEIN + WATER = GLUTEN

2 Kneading connects the gluten molecules. They make a stretchy net.

3 The yeast eats sugars in the flour. The yeast gives off carbon dioxide.

SUGAR YEAST CARBON DIOXIDE

4 Gluten traps the carbon dioxide. The gas forms bubbles.

5 The gluten net stretches as the bubbles grow. The dough rises.

CHAPTER 2 11

Letting dough rise makes bread soft and chewy. It gives it **flavor**. But this takes time. Dough may rise for minutes or hours. Some doughs are pressed down after rising. This squeezes out extra bubbles. Some breads fall if this isn't done. They bake flat. The bread does not taste as good.

An oven's heat causes the yeast to make more bubbles. The dough puffs up. The bubbles grow so big they pop. They leave holes in the bread.

DID YOU KNOW?

When dough reaches 120 degrees Fahrenheit (49 degrees Celsius), yeast dies. The dough stops rising.

CHAPTER 2

The oven's heat bakes the bread. It forms a **crust**. Soon the bread is ready to eat!

DID YOU KNOW?

There are many types of bread. Some of the most popular are white, whole grain, sourdough, rye, and naan. Yum!

CHAPTER 2　17

CHAPTER 3
LET'S BAKE!

You can make bread in a bag. Ask an adult for help. All you need is a handful of ingredients!

BREAD IN A BAG

INGREDIENTS
½ teaspoon (1.5 grams) yeast
1 teaspoon (4 g) sugar
½ teaspoon (3 g) salt
1 cup (125 g) all-purpose flour
½ cup (118 milliliters) water

KITCHEN TOOLS
1 zip-close 1-quart bag
nonstick baking sheet

START WITH THESE STEPS:

1

Measure all dry ingredients. Add them to the bag. Seal it tightly. Shake to mix well.

2

Add the water. Squeeze out any extra air in the bag. Then seal it. Squish and rub the bag until everything is wet. There should be no lumps.

CHAPTER 3   19

3

Lay the bag flat. Set it somewhere at room temperature. Turn the bag over once every hour. What changes do you see?

4

After five hours, take the dough out of the bag. Shape it into a loaf. Set it in the center of a nonstick baking sheet.

CHAPTER 3

5

Have an adult preheat the oven to 350°F (177°C). Bake the dough for about 45 minutes.

6

The bread should be light brown on top before taking it out. Wait for it to cool. Then enjoy!

CHAPTER 3

ACTIVITIES & TOOLS

TRY THIS!

MAKE SODA BREAD

Soda bread calls for baking powder and baking soda as rising agents instead of yeast. Find out how they make a different kind of bread with this fun baking activity!

What You Need:
- 2 cups (250 g) all-purpose flour
- ¼ cup (50 g) sugar
- 2 teaspoons (9 g) baking powder
- ½ teaspoon (2 g) baking soda
- 1 egg
- ½ cup (115 g) sour cream
- ½ cup (118 mL) milk
- bowl
- nonstick baking pan

1. Mix the dry ingredients together in a bowl.
2. Add the egg, sour cream, and milk. Mix.
3. Put the dough onto a nonstick baking pan.
4. Have an adult preheat the oven to 350°F (177°C). Bake the dough for about 40 minutes. The bread should be light brown on top. Let it cool, and then enjoy!

GLOSSARY

carbon dioxide: A gas made of carbon and oxygen with no color or smell.

crust: The crisp, outer layer of bread.

flavor: Taste.

gluten: A substance created from flour that gives bread its shape.

grains: The small, hard seeds of wheat, corn, rye, or other cereal plants.

ingredients: Items used to make something.

knead: To work and press a substance with the hands.

molecules: The smallest units that chemicals can be divided into.

proteins: Nutrients that are found in all living things and are necessary for life.

rising agent: A substance used to help baked goods rise.

starch: A kind of carbohydrate found in grains and many vegetables.

ACTIVITIES & TOOLS 23

INDEX

bake 4, 5, 8, 13, 17, 21
bubbles 8, 10, 11, 13, 14
carbon dioxide 8, 11
crust 17
dough 4, 7, 8, 10, 11, 13, 14, 20, 21
flour 5, 6, 7, 11, 18
gluten 7, 10, 11
grains 5, 6, 17
ingredients 5, 18, 19

knead 7, 11
oven 14, 17, 21
proteins 6, 7, 11
rises 4, 8, 10, 11, 13, 14
rising agent 5
starch 6, 7
sugars 7, 8, 11, 18
types 17
yeast 5, 8, 11, 14, 18

TO LEARN MORE

Finding more information is as easy as 1, 2, 3.
1. Go to www.factsurfer.com
2. Enter "bread" into the search box.
3. Choose your book to see a list of websites.

ACTIVITIES & TOOLS